The Road Taken

(Her Heart Heals Quietly Book 1)

Jacquinita A. Rose

Grown Folks' Publishing

Cover Design: Extended Imagery

Copyright © 2014 Jacquinita A. Rose

.

Disclaimer

ISBN-13:978-1-944167-17-2 (Paperback)
EISBN:978-1-944167-04-2
Library of Congress Control Number: 2016961142

DEDICATION

This book is dedicated to those who whether by choice or circumstances of life find themselves on a road not easily traveled.

Live! Love! Learn!

.

CONTENTS

ACKNOWLEDGMENTS

Thank you to "you" for reading this book, for the countless hours of encouragement and for your continued support of the 'Her Heals Quietly Series' Project.

CHAPTER ONE

I took the road to the left. I wasn't sure where it would lead. But I knew I wasn't going to take the road to the right because that would lead me straight back to town. That was the place I was trying to get the farthest away from. With the divorce now finalized and everything divided up appropriately, such as it was, I felt the need to run far, far away. There was nothing left for me here except questions and people trying to figure out the right words to say to comfort me and others just curious to find out what happened.

After all, James and I were the perfect couple. We lived in the perfect neighborhood. Our friends were pillars of the community and we regularly attended our local Church of Christ. So, how could this have happened? Divorce was unheard of. They say there must have been signs. I don't know if there were. Who looks for the signs that their marriage is over? I certainly didn't. I don't believe James did either. Sometimes, I think we spent so much time being perfect that we forgot how to be human.

The sound of the honks from the vehicles piling up behind me jolted me from my musings. My brain was too full of memories, flashbacks, and what ifs to focus. Right now my most important decision was trying to decide whether I should turn left to get out of this place or to turn around and go back home; whatever that meant, given that my notion of home no longer existed. After several more glaring horns and not so friendly hand gestures from the people going around me, I decided to turn left away from town, away from here; it was the only place left to go.

You really don't realize how long or large your town or state is until you are taking the trip to leave it. I think it took at least 5 hours to reach the border. I headed north, stopping only once or twice to fill up the truck with gas and to use the bathroom. It was dark now, my only company the long line of trucks headed to only God knows where.

The quick look at the gas hand lying close to "E" and the sound of my rumbling stomach let me know it was time to stop. I pulled into the second gas station. I passed by the first one which resembled a bad horror movie. It had a dimly lit parking lot and a faded handwritten sign which read "unleaded only" which made me uneasy.

The second gas station looked pretty safe; as safe as you can be at two o'clock in the morning. I pulled into the first empty stall. I looked around to be sure of my surroundings. I was a woman traveling alone, so I can never be too careful. Comfortable that I was okay, I pulled my credit card out of my wallet and quickly slid my purse under the front driver seat. Like I said, you can never be too careful. I got out and walked to the back of the truck to open the gas can. I lifted the gas handle to see another handwritten sign which read "cash only". Great! This meant I would have to go inside. I didn't have any cash on me. And I wasn't comfortable trying to take out cash this early in the morning. I was hoping to find a fast food restaurant nearby to get a bite to eat. I stared at the sign again. I was debating whether to just go somewhere else or to take my chances and to go inside.

I took a look at the highway maybe 40 feet from the gas station where I was standing. It was dark with minimal traffic. I pictured myself running out of gas and the vision that came to mind scared me. No, I don't think it wise to try and go elsewhere. I had no choice but to go inside. I reluctantly put my card back in my wallet and pulled my jacket closer to me and ventured inside the gas station.

The lights were bright. Initially, I thought the store was empty. No one was visible as I looked around for an attendant. However, I heard "morning ma'am" coming from a voice to my left. I turned to see an elderly man who looked as though he should have been somewhere enjoying retirement, not working the 2 AM shift in an all-night gas station. He was wearing freshly ironed slacks with perfect creases. His shirt was clean with a polo-style collar. I would have thought he walked right off the golf-course.

I watched as he quickly walked from the potato chips he was straightening up to behind the counter. I found myself staring at him. He had a familiar face, the type of face that you've seen someplace before but can't recall where. "How can I help you?," He pleasantly asked with a cheerful voice. I was exhausted. How could he be so cheerful this time of morning?

"I need to fill up, please," I said as I handed him my credit card.

"Oh, ma'am, I'm sorry our machine is down. We can only take cash," He said, handing me back my card.

I was tired, hungry, and needed to use the bathroom. My patience was gone. "Sir, its two o'clock in the morning. I don't have cash; I have my card!" I said, waving in front of his face. Despite my childlike antics he remained unmoved and still had the pleasant smile on his face.

"Sorry ma'am I don't make the rules I just follow them." The machines are down and I can only accept cash," he said still smiling.

Which explains why he was here instead of at home, I thought to myself.

I didn't pay attention to him when I came in but now I noticed he wore a name tag which read 'Jim'.

"Jim, I do not have cash; I only have my card," I stressed again. Well, actually I did have $10 hidden in my wallet for emergencies. But $10 wasn't enough to fill a 24-gallon gas tank. Jim looked at me and then looked at my card and let out a sigh. "I wish I could help you ma'am but cash only."

"Do the restrooms work?" I asked.

"Oh, yes, I just cleaned them about an hour ago." Jim said, clearly pleased with himself.

I turned around and look for the restroom sign. Seeing none, I turned back to Jim. Anticipating my question Jim said, "Down the hall past the money machine on your right." "Thank you," I replied. I looked at the door with a hand drawn woman on the bathroom door.

I used the sleeve of my jacket to open the door, I wasn't sure of the sanitary habits of the previous occupants of the women's restroom. I was taken aback by the freshly cleaned floors. The toilet looked brand-new. A lone stemmed flower in a slender lavender vase sat on the small shelf next to the paper towel holder. Not only did the bathroom look clean and smell clean, it was clean. However, not one to take chances, I still made a cover seat of toilet paper before I sat down.

Having completed my business, I washed my hands using two squirts of the large bottle of coconut-shea scented hand soap which smelled wonderful. This was not the bathroom of a road side gas station. It deserved to be in someone's home. I would definitely make a point to stop at this gas station on my way back. I paused for a moment to glance at my reflection in the mirror. That's right I wasn't coming back.

"Are you all right?" The voice asked from the opposite side of the door.

"I'm fine, thank you." I replied. I emerged to find Jim standing at the bathroom door with a worried look on his face.

"Sorry about that, I was admiring your bathroom," I said, running my fingers through the top of my hair.

"Oh yes, Ms. Connie always keeps a clean bathroom," Jim said, getting misty-eyed.

"Well, when you see Ms. Connie please tell her I said thank you for taking such good care of the bathroom."

"I will. I will, when I see her," Jim said as he paused and smiled and turned and walked down the hall and back behind the register.

"How far to the next gas station?," I asked Jim.

"Well since, Jake's place is closed; that's the next one after this, I'd say you got about another hundred miles or so" Jim replied matter-of-factly.

"Okay, thank you" I said, zipping up my jacket preparing to walk out the door.

"Ma'am, what about your gas?" Jim asked.

"As I said, I don't have any cash. So, I'll just have to make it to the next one." I said with a smile.

"Well, how much gas have you got?" Jim asked, his eyes clearly reflecting the uncertainty of my decision to try and make it to the next gas station.

"I'm sure I've got enough to make it to the next one. Thank you" I said while running out the door. Jim was saying something to me. But I didn't have the time to listen. I was drained and I needed to get to wherever I was going. I put the key in the ignition and started the truck. I pressed the button to the panel display to see how many miles I had left in the truck before I would run out of gas. The panel display showed that I only had 61 miles to empty. Jim had said that the next gas station was 100 miles away. I silently said a prayer that God would allow my truck to make it to the next station. I really should have gone back inside and asked for some gas. But my pride wouldn't let me; it'd taken a beating over the last few months. And so whether for lack of wisdom, stupidity, pride or a combination of all of three I continued on my journey down the road to the next gas station.

With one last look at Jim standing in the door of the gas station, I put on my turn signal and merged onto the highway. There wasn't another vehicle in sight. I owned the road. My thoughts continued to wander back-and-forth from yesterday to how clean the gas station bathroom was that I just left. About 5 minutes into my drive I noticed in my rearview mirror headlights coming up on the back of me moving rather fast. I sped up not sure of the intent of the driver. It could've been some lunatic or worse some drunk driver or perhaps someone trying to attack me. I'd been watching too much of the criminal shows on TV. I think my mind tried to get away from me. But, I still didn't like how fast those lights were coming up behind me. I didn't notice any flashing blue or red lights so I knew it wasn't a police officer or ambulance. I just got this funny feeling. I didn't know what it was. I was out here by myself and there was no one I could call.

I was out here alone. I wasn't going to be stupid and wait around to find out if it was the police; he or she could just give me a ticket. I wasn't going to stop out here in the middle of nowhere. They'd never find my body out here. I pressed hard on the accelerator. For some reason the truck wasn't responding. Actually rather than speeding up the truck was slowing down. Despite the fact I was decelerating I maneuvered the truck to the side of the road. The next thing I knew I was coming to a complete stop. "Oh, Lord, keep me safe, I prayed out loud. I didn't want to be the next episode of some missing person's show. I really need to stop watching those shows. I was beginning to dramatize my situation to the point I was really scaring myself. Besides, it was probably a police officer. I wasn't taking any chances. I reached for the bottle of mace that I kept in my glove compartment.

So, far I'd never had the need to use my bottle of mace which was why it was still unopened. I quickly tore open the container and held the bottle down beside my leg. My finger was positioned on the spray nozzle. I was silently praying to God that the bright lights of the vehicle would pass me by. I was hoping that it was just my imagination trying to get the best of me and nothing more. I was wrong. I glanced in my rear-view mirror to see the bright lights now stopped behind my truck. My prayer went unanswered. I reached for my cell-phone to dial 911. I had no signal. I wanted to be afraid. But I had no time for that. I wasn't going to be a victim. I was ready to fight. Spray first, think later.

I heard the knock on my window. "Ma'am. Ma'am?" I heard the voice ask. It sounded like a man's voice. I continue to look forward. I figured whoever this idiot was knocking on my window wouldn't harm me because I wasn't looking at him. I made sure my doors were locked. I pressed the automatic door lock again for reassurance. I turned to the window and noticed no one was there. Was I going crazy? Was I hearing voices? I looked behind me through the rearview mirror to see a figure standing next to the back of the truck.

It was hard to see who it was because of the bright lights shining from the back. They looked like truck lights. I closed my eyes and prayed again "Lord, help me." I was prepared to spray whoever this stranger was. I wasn't prepared to die.

"Ma'am, Ma'am? It's me, Jim from the gas station." I heard the voice say standing outside my window. I opened my eyes. It was Jim. I slowly rolled down my window just enough to see him. "Jim, what are you doing out here?" I hollered. Jim didn't realize how close he'd come to getting maced. Besides, I still couldn't figure out why I felt like I could trust Jim. That unnerved me more than the fact I was about to mace an old man.

"Well, I was talking to Ms. Connie. She and I thought you probably needed some gas. So, I brought you some." Jim said as he held up a large red gas can. Jim was sporting that ridiculous smile. Jim seemed like a nice old man. But nice old-men could be just as dangerous as nice young ones.

Although, I didn't detect any danger from Jim, there was still something peculiar about him. I mean, who follows someone in the middle of the night, just to give them gas. I wasn't going to take any chances finding out. I locked my doors again. I could see through the side-view mirror, Jim pouring gasoline in the gas tank. Next, Jim went back to his vehicle and got another gas-can.

Jim and I were the only ones out here. I hadn't seen another car or truck for at least 30 minutes. I checked my cell-phone again and I still didn't have a signal. To top it off, now I needed to go to the bathroom badly.

Tap, tap, I heard at my window. "Ma'am, I put about 10 gallons in. That should be more than enough to get you on down the road to the next main station. There's a truck stop about an hour and a half drive from here. Don't stop 'til you get there." Jim said as he walked back to his truck. I waited until I saw Jim get back in his truck. I put the keys in my ignition and she started right up.

Putting on my left blinker, I merged back onto the highway. I watched in my rearview mirror until Jim's bright lights emanating from his truck were enveloped by the darkness of the highway. Again I was alone. There was no one on the road but me.

I was still a little rattled by what just happened. I mean does this really happen in real life? It must because it just happened to me. I was tired, hungry, and desperately needed a bathroom and a shower. Fortunately, I was the only one in the truck, so the smell of the road consuming the truck was endured only by me. I just trusted a complete stranger with my safety. Thinking back over my life, I guess I had a thing for trusting complete strangers. I married one.

CHAPTER TWO

I was about five miles out from the truck stop Jim told me about. An hour and a half can pass by quickly when your mind is wandering. I think I was driving on automatic. The lights had all become a blur. With only a few trucks passing by the darkness was my friend. So, the Vegas style lights of the truck stop were a welcome sign. I was tired and needed to rest. I was having a hard time keeping my eyes open. I caught myself swerving a couple of times.

Thankfully, there were no other drivers on the road. I saw the sign "Exit 169". As tired as I was the sight of that exit sign reenergized me. I pictured hot food and a warm bed.

The truck stop was busy. There were 18-wheelers, two wheelers, and vehicles of every kind. From the look of the license plates every state was represented. I was hoping that I didn't run into anyone I knew. My hair was a mess. I hadn't bathed or brushed my teeth in hours. I emerged from my truck and stretched my legs. I was stiff and sore.

Somehow the crisp early morning air brought me new vigor. Although I was completely drained the air hitting my face made me believe I was wide awake and ready to conquer the world. Of course, that was only false hope. I would have slept right there in the parking lot if weren't for the fact it was unsafe and possibly illegal.

I did a couple more stretches and bent over to touch my toes. I was trying to relieve the numbness in my legs and back. Too many hours of sitting had me stiff as a board. I would definitely need to soak in the tub tonight. After a quick survey of my surroundings to ensure that all was safe, I locked the truck and went inside. I walked each of the aisles trying to find something that would ease my hunger. Unfortunately, I was too tired to decide on anything. I selected a bottle of chocolate milk. I saw in a television documentary that it was a favorite of athletes. I did a quick circle of the snack and chips aisles. Seeing nothing that appeased me, I settled for my bottle of chocolate milk and headed to the register.

"Will this be all?" The attendant asked as I placed the bottle of milk on the counter.

I still needed to find a hotel. And not being familiar with the area, I thought it best to ask. "Well, can you suggest a hotel for the night?" I asked, as I handed my only $10 bill to the attendant. I wanted to avoid another incident with my credit card, at least for now.

"This late, your best bet would be the Motel 9 or Connie's next door. They always have openings," The attendant said as she scanned the barcode on the side of my bottle of chocolate milk.

"Did you say Motel 9?" I asked.

"Yes, Ma'am. They've got the best deal in town. Their rooms are only $39.99." "Well what about Connie's?" I asked pointing next door.

"Ma'am you look like you would prefer something more up to date," The attendant said as she was ringing up my total. I was too exhausted to determine if the attendant was attempting to insult me or if she was simply stating the obvious. I had other battles to fight; this would not be one of them.

"Okay, thank you," I replied, taking my change and bottle of milk. I have never stayed in a hotel that was cheap as $39.99 a night, let alone anything called "Motel 9." I mean, that's where drug dealers and prostitutes stayed. I didn't want anyone to mistake me for one of them.

Conveniently located inside the truck stop was a sandwich shop. I went in and sat down. It felt good to be sitting somewhere besides the steering wheel on my truck. I pulled out my cell-phone. My immediate task was to find a decent room for the night. I searched the internet on my phone. The results were not promising. The next respectable four-star hotel was 80 miles away. Motel 9 was fifteen miles away. I looked outside. I could not drive another mile nor take the chance of causing an accident. It seemed Connie's Motel would be my rest stop for the night.

I quickly gulped down the last of my chocolate milk and bite of my sandwich. I considered myself to be nutritionally sound. Normally, I would not eat a sandwich from a truck stop, but hunger makes you do some strange things. My stomach was satisfied. The growling noises coming from my stomach had subsided. Now I needed to get some sleep. I walked over to the motel. I went into the lobby to find that it wasn't so bad. The chairs in the lobby looked as though curtains had been used to form the coverings. The furniture had been purchased from a discount store or a grandma's yard sale but otherwise it was clean and matched in design. Besides, I wanted a hot shower and a warm bed; the decor of the lobby was of no importance to me tonight. Perhaps, I would rethink my decision to stay in the morning. However, now my body did not care. It only required soap and water and a place to lie down.

I gently tapped the bell sitting on the front counter. While I waited for the front desk clerk to emerge, I could already feel the warm water cleansing my body. I imagined myself submerged in the welcoming warmth of the bed. I was about to tap the bell again when the front desk clerk appeared.

"May, I help you?" He asked looking none too pleased that I had disturbed him from his apparent slumber.

"Yes, I'd like a room for the night. And would you have housekeeping deliver some extra towels, please." I continued.

"Our rates are $39.99 per night. Please fill out the card first. Also, Housekeeping is out for the evening. The housekeepers will be in at 9am. Will this be cash, Visa®, or MasterCard®?"

"Neither, I'm using this one and it's just as good as those," I said as I handed him my card.

"Oh, I'm sorry, Ma'am, but we only accept the two major credit cards or cash," The clerk said, pausing from his typing.

"Well, this is the only one I have," I said, clearly irritated by his blatant disregard for my credit card.

"Ma'am, we have an atm if you would like to use cash. There is however an additional deposit of $100 required for incidentals."

"No, I don't want to use cash. I want to use my credit card!"

"Ma'am, I don't make the rules. I follow them." The desk clerk said, unmoved by the fact I did not have the money to pay for the room.

Reaching across the counter, I grabbed my card. "You know I don't have to put up with this!" I said, standing up straight. Clearly he didn't know who he was fooling with. "I'd like to speak to the manager right now. Let's see what he has to say about this!"

The desk clerk paused for a moment. He looked like he was getting ready to say something smart. That's all I needed. I was looking for someone to blame. It might as well be him. I glared back at him wishing he would say it. Say what was on his mind. Instead, he looked at me and said, "Ma'am it seems to me you've had a rough night. This one's on the house. Here's your key. Checkout's at noon. But you can stay a little longer if need be."

I stared at the key in my hand. By the time I looked back up to say thank you, the desk clerk was gone. I stood in the lobby for a moment trying to process what just happened. Someone one else might have thought it was an angel watching over me. But I didn't know what to think anymore. If it was an angel watching why didn't he watch sooner?

There'd be enough time for questioning later. Right now I was glad to have a place to sleep. I quickly exited the motel lobby for fear the desk clerk would change his mind and return for the key. *Room 102.* I searched the hallway until I came to 102. Strange it was placed near the stairwell which was odd given the room number next to it was 115. I put the key in the door and turned the knob. $39.99 was not enough to get a room with an electronic key.

The décor of the room looked like it hadn't changed in 50 years. It had a table with one chair, a microwave large enough to warm a small cup of coffee, and a bed with one pillow. I checked inside the drawer next to the bed. It was empty; looks as though $39.99 was not enough for a little green Bible either. The one painting on the wall enveloped the room. It was the standard trees in Fall intertwined with gold, red, and copper leaves. The painting was out of place for the room. Perhaps it had been placed there as an afterthought.

I pressed down on the bed with my fingertips. I wanted to be sure the mattress would be strong enough to support me. I debated whether to pull back the covers or simply sleep on top of the blanket. I decided on the latter as I was too drained to check for bed bugs. I picked up the pillow from the bed and turned it over in my hands. It felt almost empty as if the stuffing had been taken out and replaced with a small bag of cotton balls. When I laid my head on it I could feel my hand underneath.

I was too tired to undress or remove what make-up I had left on my face. I stretched out across the bed. It was uncomfortable but it was better than sleeping outside in the back seat of my truck. When I turned over I got a whiff of the blanket. It smelled like a towel that had been in the closet too long. I let out a sigh trying to relax my nerves. The room was free. Still, I'd paid too much. After two tosses and four turns, I sat up on the side of the bed. No matter how hard I tried I couldn't stop the thoughts in my mind. I looked around the room trying to take it all in. It was a far cry from three days ago when I'd been sleeping in a custom designed adjustable bed with memory foam pillows. Today, though, here I was in a room that looked like a scene from a halfway house in the 1950s. I couldn't have imagined this in my worst nightmare.

I don't remember when I fell asleep, but I awoke to the sun shining through the one inch gap in the curtain. The last thing I could recall was sitting on my bed contemplating my fate. My mind was willing to go on for hours but my body had had enough. I lay on the bed a few moments longer trying to gather myself. Was I dreaming or was I really here? With my eyes still closed, I used my hand to feel beside me. The covering on the bed felt rough in comparison to my usual thick downy covering. I raised the tip of the sheet to my nose and sniffed. I did not detect the scent of my favorite lavender fabric softener. I listened for a moment. I could not hear the sound of James' snoring. I slowly lifted my eyebrows then opened my eyes. I was still here.

I take comfort in my dreams. Sometimes they help me deal with the surrealism of my reality. There was a comfort for me in knowing what was expected of me on Monday, Tuesday, Wednesday, Thursday, Friday, Saturday, and Sunday. Each day served a purpose. Each day had meaning. Now, I don't know how to begin my days or how to end my nights.

CHAPTER THREE

Over the past week or so at this motel my life had become a new routine. I would get up, drink my cup of honey green tea and walk next door to the so-called 'fast food' restaurant which had become my primary source of entertainment until dinner which I would eat in my motel room. I enjoyed listening to the stories exchanged between the truckers passing time until their next haul. I found it amusing to watch the passersby who'd stopped for an afternoon meal staring at great length over the chalk-written menu board which only had three items: chicken and dressing (no, not turkey), meatloaf and corn, and fried catfish. The only green vegetables were green beans.

The desk clerk was true to his word. I've been here almost two weeks and he hadn't asked for any form of payment. I kept my suitcase in my truck just in case, only taking out what clothing and toiletries I needed for that day.

Here, at Connie's Motel, 380 miles north of where I was two weeks ago, I learned to sleep fully clothed. I felt unclean the first night. The next night was okay, because I slept in a constant state of "ready-to-leave." The initial shock of my divorce hadn't worn off. I was still wearing the gold band on my left finger. Oh, I should have taken it off months ago, but I had held out hope and faith. I let out a heavy sigh. As I surveyed my surroundings, I realized I was paying a heavy price for "free." This room was consuming me. I had planted the seed of misery and doubt in this room, and now I was reaping ten-fold.

I had to get out of here. I was losing sight of the bright golds, crimson reds, and harvest greens of the oversized painting that hung on the wall. Since coming here that painting had become my focal point, a measure of my sanity. However, the colors were beginning to fade or maybe it was me. The vibrancy of the colors was less apparent. When I looked at the painting I could now make out the dinginess of the grey paint in the wall behind it. I hadn't noticed it before. I was falling into darkness while desperately clinging to the light. My mind was weakened. I mentally wandered in and out of scenes of despair. I had promised myself that I would never be divorced. I would always be *Mrs.* Cheryll Ann Johnson. I would be one of those women who could proudly proclaim they'd been married 50 years. I'd have pictures, parties, family, and memories to show for it. But there'd be no parties, no pictures, no family; only memories I couldn't erase. Perhaps it was my pride that brought me here.

"Stop it! Just stop it!" I yelled to the emptiness of the room. I was tired of bathing in self-pity. I wore it like body lotion. My self-pity had seeped into the pores of my skin. I was disgusted and nauseated by the depth of my unbelief. James always said between the two of us I was the optimist. Where was my optimism now? "Father, forgive me," I humbly prayed. I had let myself travel too far down this path. I needed God to bring me out.

I raised my hands up to the sides of my face and I gently rubbed my head moving up to my temples. I needed a distraction. I needed to write. Years ago, I used to write every day. I stopped when I started seriously dating Mr.

James Johnson.

At the time, James did not believe in allocating time to people or activities which had little or no return on his investment in them. Although, I loved writing I found being with James much more exciting and intriguing. At seventeen, having no experience with men, James was like my fantasy come to life.

So, my dream of becoming a writer, along with my yellow writing pads, become part of the large stack of boxes which, until recently, occupied the back wall of our two-car garage. I peered out of my motel window. It came to me like an epiphany. That's exactly what I needed to get me out of this funk. I needed to write. Perhaps putting my thoughts on paper could help me rid myself of the physical and mental pain I was feeling.

I quickly got up and brushed my teeth and brushed my hair. There was no need for makeup as I had no one I desired to please. I grabbed a slice of pizza from the cardboard box balanced precariously in the small refrigerator next to the television. I had impeccable eating habits. It was one of the reasons why my grandmother said I had beautiful skin and great teeth. However, the eating habits and traits which I had always considered irresponsible were now part of my daily ritual. My previous night's meals were my next morning's breakfast.

Although tasty, next-morning pizza could be quite brutal on my breath. I gulped down the last bite of pizza and checked my purse for a mint. Finding none, I went into the bathroom to cleanse the taste of pizza from my mouth. After a few gargles of the alcohol laden mouthwash I wasn't quite sure if I'd just burned away the stench of pizza or perhaps it was the lining of my tongue.

I grabbed my purse from the bed and keys from the nightstand. I locked my motel room door pulling on the handle twice just to be sure it was locked. I was fortunate in that I was able to get a parking spot in front of my room. I always walked each day to the restaurant next door so my truck hadn't moved since my arrival a couple of weeks ago.

Bertha was my old faithful. A quick turn of the key in the ignition and Bertha started right up. Fortunately for me the only large retail store in town was about 20 miles east of the motel. I took the back road. I was soothed by the solitude and simplicity of the road. With five sharp curves and four maneuverable hills, I arrived at the large retail store. I knew I was only there for two things, writing pads and pens. I convinced myself I would not be swayed by cleverly displayed items I did not need or would never use. Or so I thought.

Within minutes of entering the store I found the writing pads and pens. From the vast selection of colors and designs I chose writing pads with inspirational words and phrases to motivate me as I wrote. Despite my protests I was in fact swayed to spend an additional $50 and 45 minutes to purchase knickknacks which would only occupy space in my truck.

Fearful, of spending any more money I raced towards the front checkout lane almost knocking over a mother and her child. "Excuse me, ma'am," I said, apologetically. About an hour later with my bank card balance $70 less, I pushed my cart through the parking lot to my truck. As I was placing my bags with nameless items in the back seat, I heard the familiar sound of the bell ringer and saw the red container. Strange, I didn't notice him when I came out the door. They were starting earlier this year.

I looked towards the front door of the store. Should I go back and put some money into the red container? This is so out of character for me. I always donate. I looked again at the red container then looked away. There were things I always did but circumstances changed. I really need to write.

Back at the motel I unloaded my items. I placed a cup of water in the small microwave. I splurged and bought two types of tea, regular green tea and honey earl-gray green tea. The motel provided coffee. I love the smell of fresh roasted coffee beans but I loathe the taste of coffee. It reminds me of watered-down dirt. I heard the beep of the microwave, so different from the singing of the teakettle I kept on my stove back home. How foolish of me to continue to torment myself. There I go again with that word,' home'. Connie's Motel is my home now. I plop the teabag in the mug of hot water. It has been a while since my last cup of

Jacquinita A. Rose

tea so I add another tea bag for good measure. The hibiscus honey scented steam emanates from the cup and penetrates my nostrils. The aroma is breathtaking.

It was time to write. I sat on the bed and perched myself up against the headboard. I began with one of my old visualization exercises to get my mind in the mood. I closed my eyes. I pictured myself walking barefoot through a field covered with white lilies. I like how they feel beneath my feet. I hold that image in my mind.

After about 30 seconds I picked up my pen and began to write. Pages and pages of words, sentences, and paragraphs poured from my mind. I could not stop it. It was like a faucet that could not be turned off. Several hours, several pages, and three pens later I was spent. I laid my head down on my pillow and I slept. I slept as though I hadn't slept for a lifetime.

When I awoke sometime later something was different. I blinked repeatedly to familiarize myself with the darkness of the room. The midnight sun played peek-a-boo through the opening in my curtain. I lay there for a few seconds just staring at the moon. I purred and stretched like a wife whose husband has just fulfilled her long-forgotten needs. *I hadn't felt this good in a long time,* I thought, smiling to myself. I quickly sat up in my bed and turned to check that I was in the room alone. The space beside me was empty. I had no desire to add fornication to my list of sins this past week. I placed my hand on the empty space beside me. The moon's light shining on my wedding band caused it to glow. "Oh, James did we do the right thing?" I quietly asked myself.

I paused as if expecting some reply. I received none. I was surrounded by a moat of papers. They must have fallen off the bed during my sleep. I'm glad I remembered to write the page numbers on each page. In hindsight that was an excellent idea given the fact I needed to now organize the papers haphazardly arranged around the base of my bed.

I was enjoying the feeling of the bed. I loved just lying in it. The bed had softened up since my first night. I wish I were telepathic I would use my mental powers to organize the papers now strewn across the floor. But my telepathic powers were at zero, so I had no choice but to get out of bed and organize them myself.

The room had a small table with one chair. Once I collected all the papers from the floor, I carried them to the table and set them down. I arranged the papers by page number. It was time to read them. I started with page one, carried up and down by the dark emotions reaching out at me. I had to stop reading. I needed a cup of tea. But I could not put the papers down. They were glued to my hand. Who could have written such bold angry words? I, who have been blessed beyond measure? I read the pages I had written, through and through. Once I finished, I lay them down on the table and I began to cry.

I cried for the woman woven into these pages. She was angry and blamed God. I cried for the harsh reality of the truth staring back at her. She was miserable and couldn't hide it. I cried for the woman who'd forgotten that God so loved her that he sacrificed his only begotten son. I cried for the woman who had become so consumed by her grief that she forgot the joy of her blessings. I cried for me. I had run so far and so long avoiding uncomfortable questions, but I hadn't escaped me.

I recalled when I helped two of my closest friends while they were struggling with the loss of their husbands; one by the stroke of a judge's pen and another to cancer. Then, it was easy for me to comfort and console; to help them bear their crosses. But now, I found it almost impossible to bear my own. The truth was I had been a hypocrite. I advised others to pray and to stay close to God in their time of trouble, when I tried to run from Him.

I got up from the bed and walked over to the curtain to look outside. The moon was full and close to my fingertips. I pressed my hand against the window pane trying to touch it. I stared at the moon and looked back at the stack of papers I had just read. Thinking of the woman trapped within those pages, I silently prayed "Lord, please don't let me be her."

I stood looking out into the night sky through my motel window until the cold emanating from the window became uncomfortable. It was time for tea. I closed the curtain and walked over to the microwave. I put the mug of water in the microwave to heat it up and I took my tea out of the cabinet next to the stove. This was going to be a three tea bags night.

Later that night, I found myself sitting in the truck-stop restaurant next to the motel. I continued to meditate on my writing, while enjoying sips of peppermint tea. The world was a much bigger place than me. And yet I have reduced it to be 20 x 15 space of my motel room. I finished my tea and headed back to my room. The pages were still lying on the table where I'd left them. I decided to take a shower to help me fall asleep. The warm water washed away the dirt from my body but it could not cleanse the thoughts of my mind. The woman reflected in the pages I've written is dark without hope. She clothed herself in bitterness and slept with despair. I could not be her; I would not be her. *Perhaps I had been possessed*, I thought to myself. There was no way those 50 pages had come from me. They spewed hatred, doubt, and mistrust. My life up until recently was full of joy. I went to the best schools. Growing up my family lived in one of the most prestigious neighborhoods. I grew up with love. I was surrounded by it. So how could I think such thoughts and worse write them down.

CHAPTER FOUR

I quickly gathered all the papers together. I methodically tore them into tiny little pieces. I didn't want them to be found. I have to get rid of them somehow. There was no fireplace in my motel room in which to burn them. So, the only place I could think of to get rid of the evidence of my lack of faith was to flush them down the toilet. I collected each torn piece of paper in a plastic bag and carried them to the bathroom. One by one I flushed each piece down the toilet. When I was done and satisfied that the evidence of my writing was gone, I went back into the room and sat down on the bed. I didn't want to be so concerned by anger and sorrow that it would be etched on my face. I'd seen firsthand how bitterness devours a woman's face leaving her skin dried and wrinkled, with the light stripped from her eyes.

I wanted to write because I thought it would help me. Now, it scared me. If the woman in those pages was somehow inside me, how did she get there? More importantly how would I get rid of her? I sat at the table and watched my notepad and my pen. I wanted so badly to pick up my pen and write. But what I wrote I could not control. There were no pretty flowers, and no happy endings. Perhaps, I needed to rest for a minute and gather my thoughts. I folded my arms on the table and rested my head on them for just a moment.

I awoke to the sound of alarm in my truck going off. I lifted my head from the table and listened. Someone had probably gotten too close to the driver's door. The alarm had always been sensitive. When I bought Bertha, I set the truck alarm off four times before I drove her away from the dealership. I pulled my keys from my purse and opened the curtain and pressed the red button to shut off the alarm. I watched from the window a few moments longer. Seeing no one near the truck, I closed the curtain, put keys back in my purse and sat down on the edge of the bed. I was still watching the notepad and pen lying on the table.

"I can do all things through Christ which strengthens me." I kept hearing this verse of

Scripture in my head. I knew that this was a sign from God telling me not to be afraid of a notepad and pen. If I was to heal, I had no choice but to deal with the truth: The truth about me, the truth about James, and the truth about my marriage: But greater than all of these I had to deal with the truth about my faith.

I let out a deep sigh to calm my nerves. The other voice in my head was telling me to run, to get out of here. I sat staring at my notepad and pen lying on the table challenging me to pick it up. This was a pivotal point for me. I could pick up the pen and write as if my life depended on it or I could run away fast to my next "I don't know where I'm going." I was tired of running. I walked over to the table sat down pulled the notepad close to me, picked up the pen lying beside it, and begin to write.

I am afraid although I should have no fear. I feel doubt as to why you brought me here. I looked to the light; the darkness is all I see. I love you Lord but I can't feel the love you have for me. My life is changing in ways I can't understand. Why me Lord, when I only use my life to follow your plan? Your word tells me to have faith, this will pass, and I will grow. But Lord, I can't see which way to go. My life is a dream that has gone terribly wrong. Tell me please which way, how to remain strong? I should be thankful and rejoice. But I find that I can't; I'm wrapped, consumed, by my failure, my divorce. Lord, I believed you'd given me this man to love, to honor, to cherish and to hold. Then why Lord, please tell me why, was it so easy for him to let go?

I put down my pen and pushed my chair away from the table. It was time for tea. I took a quick shower, put my hair up in a ponytail, threw on an old T-shirt and my favorite pair of jeans. I wasn't eating as much these days so I was able to easily fit in them. Comfortable with my attire, I picked up my key and touched my notepad on my way out the door.

I walked over to the restaurant. I ordered my usual, the cup of peppermint tea. My normal booth was open so I sat down. I'd been here two weeks now and I hadn't introduced myself to anyone. I hadn't even taken the time to say "hello" to the waitress who always had my tea ready when I came in or to the trucker who passes through like clockwork on Thursdays. Although he was very friendly with everyone I couldn't recall his name. I just called him the "Thursday trucker." It fit. Some example I was so busy being miserable I'd forgotten my raising, my manners and who I was professing to be. If the change was to take place it would have to start with me. I decided I'd start with at least learning the names of the waitress and of that Thursday trucker.

The waitress always refilled my tea. I think she had ESP. She knew exactly when I needed more. I looked up in time to see her headed towards my table with a hot cup of water and fresh tea bag.

"Thank you," I said smiling as she placed a fresh cup of hot water and tea bag on my table in front of me.

"Well, you're welcome," she said as she prepared to leave.

"Excuse me, ma'am, what is your name?" I asked.

"Kim Li with an "I," the waitress said with a smile.

I tried to hide the puzzled expression on my face. I did not consider myself prejudiced, stereotypical, or narrow-minded. However, the waitress had no distinctive Asian features. In fact, she had blond hair with sparkling blue eyes. As if reading my thoughts, Kim Li winked at me and said, "Everyone has a story to tell, maybe when I get some time I will tell you mine. I've got to check on my other tables. I'll be back to check on you later." Then Kim Li was gone to check on the table at the front of the restaurant.

I took another sip of the delicious peppermint tea. I became preoccupied with watching the steam rising from my cup. It was a welcome distraction from the earlier events of my "50 pages." I was interrupted by the sound of a familiar voice.

"How are you doing lovely lady?"

I looked around to find out who might be the recipient of his question. I was quite surprised to see that the Thursday trucker's question was directed at me. He had already taken the liberty of sitting down at my table in a chair directly across from me. I blushed somewhat slightly. I could only imagine my appearance given I had not applied any under-eye cream this morning. It had been quite some time since I've been referred to as a "lovely lady." I figured his vision was probably getting bad which was not a good thing being that he was an over-the-road trucker. I think I should suggest that he get his eyes checked on his next stop through town. But for now I would relish being a "lovely lady."

"Well, I won't give you permission to sit down," I said laughingly.

"Oh, I'm sorry," Thursday trucker said as he immediately stood back up.

"Stop being silly," I said not wanting to draw any attention to my table.

Seeing my discomfort the Thursday trucker sat down. "I knew there was a smile in there," he said as he rearranged the salt and pepper shakers at the end of my table. I did not like people rearranging my things. I'd experienced that too much lately. The Thursday trucker did not know me well enough to take such liberties!

I did not respond. I forgot I was

supposed to be making a change.

"So, is your peppermint tea to your liking?," He asked determined to involve me in his conversation.

Realizing that the Thursday trucker was not going to leave me alone, I joined in.

"Actually, it's quite good and the weather is quite nice," I said, anticipating that his next question would be about the weather.

"Well, I can see what the weather is for myself by looking out the window," the Thursday trucker said, frowning. "If you are trying to get rid of me you'll have to do better than that!"

This conversation was taking a wrong turn. I could clearly see that I was upsetting the Thursday trucker which was not my intent. Actually, I just wanted to know his name. I abruptly changed the subject.

"What's your name?" I asked.

"Why?" Thursday trucker responded.

"I like to know who I'm talking to," I

replied.

"Oh, so now you want to know me," Thursday trucker said, pretending to scan the menu.

"No," I replied truthfully. "I just want to know your name."

Thursday trucker put down his menu. "Why?"

I could see he was intentionally irritating. Thursday trucker was playing a game. What he didn't know was that I did not like playing games. When I asked a question I expected an answer; the right one!

"Are you going to tell me your name or not?" I asked, attempting to mask my frustration with this man. "My question was simple enough."

"Oh, so you think I'm simple now?" the Thursday trucker said, his face now stoic and unreadable.

"Of course not! I just want to know your name and you're turning my questions into some kind of drama scene." I said through gritted teeth. I was tiresome of Thursday trucker's childlike game of 50 questions.

"You're gritting your teeth. That's a bad sign. Do you know you might have a nervous condition?" Thursday trucker grinned as he leaned towards me.

Clearly, Thursday trucker was trying to rile me. For what purpose I did not know, nor did I care. I was determined he would not have the satisfaction of seeing me fall apart in front of him.

"Look, I was trying to be pleasant. However, I can see that you just want to sit there and play silly games. I will not have any part of it!" I said as I got up to leave the table. Kim Li, my waitress who usually had impeccable timing chose this exact moment to show up with another hot cup of tea.

"Sorry, Kim Li, I didn't ask for another cup of tea!" I said rather sharply.

"Don't worry, it's not for you," the Thursday trucker said as he smiled at Kim Li.

"What'd you bring me?" Thursday trucker asked Kim Li, pretending to be surprised.

"Earl Grey, hot with fresh lemon, two bags," Kim Li said and smiled.

Kim Li and the Thursday trucker held each other's gaze as she placed the cup of tea and small bowl of lemons down on the table in front of him. When Thursday trucker smiled back at Kim Lee his features softened. *Was there something going on between Thursday trucker and Kim Li?* I asked myself. I could fill the intensity of the energy around the table change. I felt like passion and love. I wanted no part of it.

"Thank you, Kim Li! That's all we need," I said, dismissing her. Kim Li quickly stepped back from the table and said, "I better go check on my other customers."

"What's your problem?!" Thursday trucker yelled at me as he leaned even closer over the table towards me.

"Lower your voice! People will hear you!" I whispered to the Thursday trucker. I considered public displays of emotions, particularly arguments, primitive and barbaric. People who engaged in such behavior were no better.

"I don't care who hears me!" Thursday trucker glared at me; his face was now bright red.

"If you're going to act like this I will not sit here and listen," I said as I turned to leave.

"Since, you're not sitting I don't see that as a problem. Why don't you go do what you do so well!" Thursday trucker said.

"And what is that?! "I asked. He didn't know anything about me.

"Running! Why don't you go run away!" Thursday trucker said as he raised his head to watch the large TV screen mounted on the wall above the restaurant.

Back in my room, I tried to figure out what was wrong with Thursday trucker. Why was he so upset? I probably would never understand men. Besides, Kim Li had interrupted our conversation. And she needed to look after her other customers anyway.

Knock! Knock! Someone was banging on my hotel room door. I wasn't alarmed given no one knew I was here. It was probably just the front desk clerk. I opened the door. I was greeted by the Thursday trucker holding a cup of hot tea. To say I was surprised was an understatement. Before I could say anything the Thursday trucker spoke.

"Here's your peppermint tea! Kim Li wanted me to bring you a fresh cup." Thursday trucker said still holding the cup of tea in his hand.

"Well thank you," I said, reaching for the cup. That was very thoughtful of Kim Li. Please tell her I said 'thank you,'" I said, reaching for the cup in his hand.

"Oh no, you don't!" Thursday trucker said as he moved the cup of tea out of my reach. "You're right Kim Li is kind, caring, and thoughtful. Something you don't understand and probably will never be. You listen and listen good! The next time you disrespect Kim Li I will throw you and your peppermint tea out of this town! Good day!" Thursday trucker said as he pushed the cup of tea in my hand and walked away. People like him were a test to my faith. Sometimes, he made me just want to go slap-happy upside his head. Of course, that was just me talking crazy. Thursday trucker looked like he could get slap-happy back. I watched him go into the motel office. Good, let him go pester someone else for a while.

I closed the door and placed my tea down on the table. I sat on the bed. Clearly, there was something mentally wrong with this Thursday trucker. I might have been a little sharp with Kim Li but I'd never disrespected her. I certainly hadn't done anything that warranted this behavior from the Thursday trucker. Besides I would see her tomorrow and apologize. Some people could be overly sensitive, although Kim Li did not strike me as the type of person. The peppermint tea sure smelled good. I walked back over to the table, picked up the cup and took a sip. Aaahh, yes, the tea was delicious. *Kim Li was definitely thoughtful,* I said to myself.

Three minutes into my cup of peppermint tea, I heard another knock at my hotel door. I guess that was probably Thursday trucker coming back to apologize but I would beat him to it. "I'm sorry," I said as I rushed to open the door. It was not the Thursday trucker. It was the front desk clerk. He was shuffling his feet. He had his hands in his pocket and would not make eye contact with me. Something must be wrong.

"Hi," I smiled. I gestured to him to come in.

"No, that's okay. I was just checking to see that everything was okay."

"No, did someone call you about the little incident that just happened? It was nothing. Don't worry it was just some rude trucker," I said, trying to reassure the desk clerk.

"Actually, I came about the room. Starting tomorrow I'll have to charge you full price for the room." He said rather reluctantly.

"Why, what happened?" I asked anxiously. I'd been here almost two weeks. I didn't have that kind of cash on hand.

"Well, that crazy, rude trucker you

mentioned is my uncle. He owns the motel. I don't know what you said or did but…"

"But what?" There was more?

"You have to have payment for the previous days you been here by tomorrow or you have to leave."

The room started spinning. I was grateful for the strength of the doorknob holding me up. "Sure." I said frozen in place.

"Are you going to be okay?" The front desk clerk asked. Concern etched on his face.

"Of course," I said with my "everything is fine" smile showing on my face. I shut the door. I'd kept my suitcase packed since I got here. So there wasn't much for me to load up except the memories of this place. In a few short days, Connie's Motel had become my home. But the fact was it was a motel so it would never really be my home. I've been asked to leave because I insulted a waitress; a waitress who unbeknownst to me meant more to the owner of the hotel than just someone who serves tea in a roadside restaurant. I should feel something. I didn't. I felt absolutely nothing at all.

CHAPTER FIVE

I checked my watch. He'd be here in fifteen minutes. He was never late. I checked my hair and my teeth in the rearview mirror. I hadn't slept at all since yesterday. No amount of make-up this morning could hide the bags under my eyes. I pretended not to notice and hoped he wouldn't either. I popped a mint in my mouth for good measure. One minute later, I noticed his spotless black Mercedes pull up behind me. I got out of the truck at the same time he was getting out of his car.

"Hi," we both said simultaneously. Due to the urgency of the matter there was no time for small talk.

"Do you have it?" I asked. "Yes," he said as he handed me a thick white envelope.

"Thank you, James," I said as I wrapped my arms around his neck and gave him a hug. We both realized I had a momentary lapse of judgment

"Be careful," James said as he gently pulled away from me.

"Why?" I asked. James smiled for a moment like he was trying to find the words to say. He didn't take long to find them.

"You always seem to find a way to mess up your blessings. Don't mess up this one," James said as he walked to his car. I watched him get in, turn right and drive away. He didn't look back.

I got in my truck and examined the contents of the envelope. Inside was a thick stack of fresh, crisp $100 bills. I counted out six $100 bills from the white envelope and put them in my wallet; that would be more than enough to cover my motel bill. I put the rest back in my purse, started up my truck, and turned left, headed back to Connie's Motel.

I pulled into the parking lot. My parking space in front of my room was available so I parked there. I found familiarity most comfortable. On the drive back I mulled over the idea of just not going back. Maybe travel to some other obscure location. That would have been easy for me to do, but I refused to give the Thursday Trucker the satisfaction.

I pushed the bell sitting on the front counter of Connie's Motel. It was midafternoon; the front desk clerk should be here.

"Hello? Hello?" I called but received no response. He must be out checking the rooms. I decided to leave him a note. I simply wrote, "I'm staying, Room 102. I'm sorry that I missed you." I left the note lying on top of his computer keyboard and headed back to my room.

Once inside, I pulled out the envelope to count how much money it contained. 28, 29, 30... There were 30, fresh-from-the-bank smelling, $100 bills including the six I took out earlier to pay for my room. I put the money back inside the envelope and pressed it against my chest. "Thank you, Lord," I said out loud.

As part of the divorce settlement James offered to pay me monthly spousal support. I did not have a steady source of income nor any immediate means of generating any. So, logic would dictate that I except James's generosity. I declined it. I have a bad tendency of letting my pride get in the way. I was determined to show James and everyone else that I could take care of myself. So far, I hadn't done the best job. I didn't have any place to go besides Connie's Motel. Well, if I was truthful with myself I did have my home that I left behind, but I really didn't want to go back there now. So I had no other option but to stay at Connie's Motel which meant I had to call James.

I needed this money to pay for the room. James was not the type to give money to anyone unless he knew the exact reason for the request. So I had to tell James everything; about Jim, the gas, Connie's Motel, Kim Li, and the Thursday trucker. James said I still had a lot to learn. I believe I've learned enough.

I glanced over at the red letters glaring on the small clock sitting on my nightstand. 30 minutes had passed since I left my note at the front desk. The clerk should be back by now. I checked again for the $600 in my wallet and headed back over to the front desk. I noticed that my note which I left earlier was gone. I tapped on the bell sitting at the edge of the front desk counter. Still no answer. "Where could he be?" I asked myself. Connie's Motel was not that large, so whatever he was doing clearly he should have been finished by now. Besides he could not have gone far because the door to the office was still unlocked. I wasn't going to stand around waiting. If I didn't know better I would think the desk clerk was hiding from me.

I still had my room key so I simply returned to my room and waited. I noted earlier that my room had been cleaned. Connie's Motel provided weekly cleaning services for guests staying longer than five days. I turned the light on and checked the bathroom. It was spotless. The only change was a slender lavender vase containing a single stem yellow rose. If I didn't know better I would have thought Jim, from the gas station down road, had been here. I leaned over and inhaled the fragrant sent of the rose. Breathtaking! Besides, Jim worked almost 100 miles away. So, I knew it couldn't be him. When I walked over to the bed, I noticed a purple piece of paper left on the pillow. I opened the note and read it: "I hope you like the room." The note was signed *Kim Li*.

The note didn't have a clear recipient. I didn't know if the note had been left for me or for the next possible occupant. I then saw another post-it-note left on the TV which read: "yes, the note was for you. Kim Li" Obviously Kim Li wanted the next guest in the room to feel welcomed.

I'd only been gone a few hours. But, I could see that the Thursday trucker did not expect me to return. He'd wasted no time in cleaning my room. I smiled when I thought how surprised he would be to find out I stayed. I sat back down on the bed and picked up the phone to call the front desk. I wanted to make sure that I paid for the room before the Thursday trucker returned. The phone rang three times. I was about to hang up when I heard a voice on the other end say "hello."

"Hello?"

"Hello, this is room 102."

"Oh, hi."

"Yes, I came by a few minutes ago to pay

for my room. But no one was there. I left you a note. Did you see it?"

"Oh, yeah, I got it. We have an emergency in another room." The front desk clerk said rather nonchalantly. I sensed that he had disregarded my note. It was probably in pieces at the bottom of his trash can. I would not give him an opportunity to dismiss me again.

"Okay. Well I will come back over now. Don't go anywhere. See you in a few seconds," I said as I hung up the phone. For the third time I went back to the office. The front desk clerk was waiting for me. For some reason he didn't wear a name tag. So I still didn't know his name. I would soon remedy that.

"Hi," I said, glad to see him. "What's your name?" I asked him. He hesitated before responding.

"I can't tell you," He replied. The clerk turned his eyes away from me as if he feared I could read his mind. Initially, I was shocked. This was a grown man acting like a child. I found his behavior ridiculous. I can only guess the reason for his secrecy.

"Why won't you tell me your name?" I asked, curious to see if my suspicions were correct.

"Would you like to pay for your room now?" He asked, avoiding my question.

"Yes," I replied as I handed him the money. I wanted to get this taken care of before the Thursday trucker returned. I was sure he's the one behind the front desk clerk withholding his name. The Thursday trucker relished playing games. I, however, do not. I checked the receipt given to me by the front desk clerk. I wanted to be sure it accurately reflected a zero balance. I smiled as I saw his name written in the left-hand corner of the receipt. His name was "John." I looked at it. He did not look like a "John." He probably typed the name there to throw me off, or perhaps not.

"Thank you, John," I said as I folded up the receipt and put it in my purse.

"You're welcome," he replied.

I'd already had enough battles with the

Thursday trucker. I wasn't going to add trying to find out the desk clerk's name to the list. Back in my room, I exhaled. Thanks to James, I had taken care of the payment for my room but there was still the issue of the Thursday trucker. Was my payment enough or would he say get out anyway? I decided not to stress anymore about him. I needed to do something more productive. Instead I chose to take a nap. I usually didn't take naps. But for some reason, I felt extremely tired.

CHAPTER SIX

Approximately two hours later I awoke to the sound of banging on the door. What now? I was trying to rest, and I didn't appreciate being interrupted.

"What is it!?" I asked aloud as I answered the door. Oh, no, not him! Today was Wednesday. What was he doing here?

"Thank you." The Thursday trucker said. I didn't think you had it in you."

I remained silent. I was tired. I would not be goaded by his shenanigans. What does his "thank you" mean anyway? I asked myself. The best he could muster was "thank you" after he scared the daylights out of me and forced me to ask James for money!

"You're welcome," I said, pretending not to care. This man drained me. He required too much energy. Kim Li had lots of energy, maybe that's why he was drawn to her. I closed my eyes for a moment hoping that this was just a dream and nothing more. I open my eyes to find him still standing there. The Thursday trucker looked as if he was waiting for me to invite him in or waiting for me to tell him to go.

"Is that all?" I asked the awkward silence flustered me more than his aggressive nature.

"For now," the Thursday trucker said as he tipped his hat.

I closed the door and leaned against it. A woman could accidentally mistake the Thursday trucker for a gentleman. I checked the time on the clock next to my bed. I sighed. I was hungry. I didn't feel like ordering pizza. I was hungry for something with more sustenance. I could hide out in my motel room but that wasn't going to appease my hunger. I wanted to avoid running into the Thursday trucker. I could only stomach so much of him. I glanced again at the clock and rubbed my stomach. My choices were hide or hunger. Given that the Thursday trucker knew where I was staying, hiding was not a real option. As such, I chose to cure my hunger.

I needed to figure out what to eat. I was

so hungry that I didn't know what to eat. I went down my list of `usual' quick go-to meals: pizza, Chinese stir-fry and burgers. But, nothing piqued my interest. So I would have to eat at the restaurant next door. At least there my choices would be limited, making it easy for me to decide what to eat.

The day was relatively warm so I didn't need a jacket. Making sure I had my room key, ID and some money, I locked my door and walked over to the restaurant and went inside. The restaurant was fuller than usual. I thought there must be a festival or something in town. I saw the flyer earlier hanging on the bulletin board in the motel office when I was paying my bill. Surprisingly, my table was open. I hurried up and sat down. I examined the handwritten chalk menu longer than usual. This time I chose meatloaf and green beans. I was hesitant to try the fried catfish. I generally did not eat fried foods anyway. I'd overheard another trucker saying he didn't eat any catfish because they were scavengers and bottom-feeders. He said you could get seriously ill from eating them. I don't know if his comments were accurate, but I wasn't going to take a chance and find out.

Yes, then meatloaf it is.

Content with my selection I looked around for Kim Li. I was ready to order. This was unusual. Kim Li always brought me my tea by now. Something wasn't right. I spotted another waitress at the table across from me. She was clearing the dishes from the previous customers.

"Excuse me, ma'am, is Kim Li here," I asked, scanning the restaurant.

"No, she's off today. But she'll be back on Thursday. Can I get you something?"

"Yes, I'd like a cup of peppermint tea, please" I said, smiling at the waitress hoping that my displeasure was not showing on my face. I became accustomed to Kim Li bringing my tea. I enjoyed routine and order. They were my strengths and my weaknesses. However being at Connie's Motel was forcing me to challenge my ideas about "routine."

"I'm going to check to be sure, but I think we are fresh out of peppermint tea," The waitress said.

How could they be fresh out of peppermint tea? Most everyone here was a coffee drinker. I was the only one who ever ordered real tea. I was addicted to peppermint tea like a drug addict needed a fix. I had to have at least two cups a day. Woe to the person who came between me and my tea. Evidently, the Thursday trucker was trying to quickly get on the wrong side of me.

Something sounded suspicious to me. First, Kim Li is conveniently off until Thursday, and now the restaurant is out of peppermint tea. This was no big mystery. Clearly, Thursday trucker was behind this. He wanted me to leave ever since the incident with Kim Li.

I saw the waitress walking back towards my table. I can only imagine what she'd heard about me from the Thursday trucker. Probably that I was going to bite her head off which was absurd. Apparently the waitress didn't know that. I saw fear in her eyes.

"I'm sorry, but we don't have peppermint tea. The restaurant has decided to discontinue it," The waitress said as she glanced down at her notepad.

"How convenient!" I muttered to myself. Sure, they didn't have peppermint tea. I bet if I walked back there to the stock room I would see a mountain of it. What the Thursday trucker didn't know was that I'd eaten in a lot better restaurants than this. I could easily take my business elsewhere.

"Okay, that's fine, thank you," I said as I slid out of the booth.

"Can I get you something else? Some coffee?," The waitress asked, appearing distressed by my getting up to leave the restaurant. They probably didn't get too many customers leaving without ordering something.

"No, that's fine. Have a nice day." I said as I walked out the door. I took in a deep breath, held it for a moment and let it go. Again the Thursday trucker was playing games with me, trying to rattle me. I would not give him the pleasure of knowing that it was working.

I looked to my left and then to my right. The Thursday trucker was probably somewhere watching. Let him watch this! I went back to my hotel room to get my jacket and my purse.

There were other places to eat. I could easily go someplace else. I pulled out of the parking stall in front of my room slowly hoping he was somewhere watching. I drove out of the motel parking lot at about two miles per hour for no particular reason. *Look Thursday trucker, I can play games too.*

CHAPTER SEVEN

I think I'd taken a wrong turn because I've driven for about 15 miles from the motel and I hadn't spotted any restaurants. Just as I was thinking about turning around and going back to my motel room to order a pizza, I saw the sign to a familiar food chain restaurant. As I pulled into the parking lot I could see that it was relatively full. I would probably have the customary 15 to 20 minute wait if the parking lot was any indication of the number of people inside the restaurant. I found a parking spot on the side of the restaurant which was fine for me. I didn't want any dings on my truck. So I had a tendency to park further away or I straddled two parking spots to ensure no one parked next to me. I found the method to be very effective. There are a lot of people with truck-envy. But judging by the large number of trucks in the parking lot I probably wouldn't have to worry about dings tonight.

The walls inside the restaurant were dark cherry wood. Maybe that was why the restaurant was equipped with lights that shown too brightly for the room. I spotted a vacant booth in the corner. I did not wait to be seated. I couldn't take the chance that someone else might get the booth instead which was rather silly seeing as I was the only person standing in line. I waved to the hostess to let her know that I have found a seat. The expression on her face let me know she was not all pleased with my apparent rudeness. I followed her gaze as she paused momentarily at the "please wait to be seated" sign next to the hostess stand. She was carrying a menu and plastic ware. She placed the plastic ware down on the table in front of me.

"Hello, ma'am, your server will be with you shortly," she said as she lay the menu down in front of me. Thank you for choosing Eclipse." The hostess then smiled and walked away but not before I saw her flush red and the slight protrusion of the vein on the side of her head. *Oh, I bet she was thankful*, I said under my breath. The veins don't lie.

I was scouring the menu, when I heard the clang of a miniature silver teapot.

"Oh, I didn't order anything," I said as I looked up from studying the menu. I recognized a familiar face. "Kim Li, what are you doing here?" I asked, excited. My initial excitement quickly turned to annoyance. If Kim Li was here that meant the Thursday trucker was probably somewhere close by. Great, what a way to spoil a great cup of tea! The Thursday trucker could easily fall off the planet and I'd be very happy. I suddenly looked around me to see if he was standing there. He was not.

"Don't worry, he's not here," Kim Li laughed.

"He who?" I asked, pretending to be ignorant of whom she was referring to.

"Come on now, don't act like you don't know who `he' is," Kim Li said, resting her hands on her hips.

"Sorry, was I that obvious?" I asked.

"Yes, you were and you are," Kim Li laughed again.

"What are you doing here?" I asked. It

never occurred to me that Kim Li worked someplace else. I just assumed the restaurant next to the truck stop was her only source of income.

"Silly, I work here," Kim Li said, pulling out her pad and pen. "So what would you like to order?"

"I don't know, Kim Li. I'm hungry, but I can't seem to pick anything." The menu at the restaurant had only three meals so it was easier to choose. But this menu before me has so many food options, cooked in so many ways, with so many sauces, that it overwhelmed me. I looked to Kim Li to help me decide.

"What do you recommend?" I asked, still flipping the pages of the menu.

"Well, the number five looks good. But, are you a little hungry or really hungry?" Kim Li asked me.

I didn't want to hurt her feelings by telling her that I generally did not eat at restaurants that had numbered specials. I was accustomed to ordering what I wanted whether it is on the menu or not. But, I was in a different place with different rules, where food was cooked and covered in sauces and the word "healthy" was not a concern. I did not want to further insult Kim Li by ordering nothing. So I chose between what appeared to be the best options, the number five or the number 10. The items on the menu appeared to be either baked in grease, fried in grease, or broiled in grease.

"I'll take the number five," I said, folding and then handing my menu back to Kim Li. My reward was a sincere, reassuring smile from Kim Li. Excellent! If Kim Li was happy then the Thursday trucker was happy, for now.

"Thank you, I'll be back with your appetizer," Kim Li said as she quickly headed towards the kitchen. Wait, I didn't order an appetizer. I would correct the mistake when Kim Li returned. While I waited for my food I took the time to ingest the atmosphere of Eclipse. I found the name to be unusual for a restaurant. To me the name 'Eclipse' was more indicative of a dance club or something like that. This must be the only restaurant for miles because the customers ranged from people in their Sunday finest to people in shorts, sundresses and flip-flops. Someone should probably let them know it would be real chilly in a few hours. I felt like I was swimming in a sea of tourists. I was so focused on my study of the patrons that I neglected to hear Kim Li bring my food. I heard the sound of someone clearing their throat.

"Here's your food," Kim Li said, placing my plate down in front of me. I was pleasantly surprised to see my broiled fish and steamed vegetables were not smothered in sauce.

"Wow, Kim Li, how'd you pull this off?" I asked, too hungry to care about manners as I took my first bite of the fresh fish. So sweet and flaky that it melted in my mouth.

"I made a special request from the chef," Kim Li said as she sat down at my table. I didn't want Kim Li to get reprimanded for sitting down while she was supposed to be working.

"Is it okay for you to sit down?" I asked, concerned that she might be fired for fraternizing with the customers.

"No, I'm fine," Kim Li said, apparently void of any concern with what the manager might do. I noticed the waitress brought Kim Li a cup of jasmine tea.

Well, please forgive my manners," I said as I devoured my plate of food. I was raised not to talk with my mouth full. But for some reason, I didn't care about manners or etiquette. I shoveled through my plate like a plow clearing away the snow after a winter storm. I came up for air once my plate was empty. I delicately wiped the sides of my mouth with my paper napkin.

"You should never let your stomach get that empty," Kim Li said sternly- clearly disturbed by my rapid consumption of my meal. She had the look of concern of someone who thinks you have a problem when in fact you don't. I'd been under quite a bit of stress lately so I didn't eat much food. I guess my body was trying to tell me in a very embarrassing way that it needed more nutrients.

"I generally don't, I said with a smile. I've just been so busy that I haven't had time to eat like I should." My explanation was not sufficient enough to soothe Kim Li's concerns.

"You continue being too busy to eat and you won't need to eat because you'll be dead," Kim Li said, strangely calm.

Kim Li was being very melodramatic as far as I was concerned. I didn't need a mother. I was a grown woman. The last thing I needed was a lecture from Kim Li. I couldn't say anything to Kim Li that might be considered disrespectful. I had already incurred the Thursday Trucker's mischievous discontent; that's all he needed was another reason to boot me out. So, I simply said "thank you." Kim Li had been sitting at my table for almost 20 minutes. Most breaks are only for fifteen. If Kim Li didn't get up soon she might be looking for a new job.

Kim Li was one of those people you really couldn't say no to. She was so genuine. She was an angel. When Kim Li waited on your table she treated you like royalty whether you ordered a cup of water or a full meal. So, how did she get mixed up with someone like the Thursday Trucker? Before I unraveled that mystery, I wanted to know how she got the name 'Kim Li'. It would be rude for me to come out and ask, but if I didn't find out soon I could picture myself asking something embarrassing like "So, Kim Li, how did you get your name?"

"I thought you'd never ask," Kim Li said, winking at me about her porcelain white teacup.

Great! Just great! I did not mean to say that out loud, I said to myself. I watched the reaction on Kim Li's face. Kim Li has such beautiful skin; must be genetics. She is always at peace I could tell it by the look of constant relief that was always on her face.

"Lean closer," Kim Li said. I leaned closer. My anticipation was growing. I really wanted, no I needed to know about her name. I had formulated the origin of her name in my imagination. Now was my chance to see if my imagination matched her reality.

"Well, when I was a kid I could not pronounce my name, Kimberly. I would always say "Kim Lee." My parents could never figure out why it was hard for me to pronounce the 'b' in my name. So, everyone just called me Kim

Lee. When I got old enough I changed my name to Kim Li, with an `I'. It sounded more exotic. That's it," Kim Li said as she smiled and leaned back in her seat.

"That's it!?" I asked. I had built up these outrageous scenarios in my head. What a let-down! Kim Li sensed my disappointment.

"You know sometimes the mystery of the search can be more exciting than the find itself," Kim Li said as she sipped the last ounce of her jasmine tea. Kim Li winked at me and walked back behind the counter. She washed her hands in the small sink behind the register. I continued shaking my head. I'd let my imagination get the better of me. My mind had run rampant with scenarios of intrigue and mystery; a possible adoption or maybe someone she'd admired had influenced her to change her name. All along her name was Kim Li for no other reason than she wanted it to be.

I waited for the waitress to bring me my check. I continued watching Kim Li while I waited. I could not explain my fixation with Kim Li. Maybe it was because she reminded me of my favorite teacher in elementary school.

Kim Li greeted the customers, poured tea, water and coffee. I saw her go back and forth in the kitchen to check on customers' orders. Kim Li moved around the restaurant with the confidence and familiarity of an owner. Of course, Kim Lee was not the owner. I'm sure the actual owner was very pleased with Kim Li's work. She is an extraordinary waitress who gives excellent advice.

The young lady assigned to my table finally brought my check. She placed it face down on the table along with a serving of tiramisu and a cappuccino. Kim Li knew I didn't like coffee. But this was not Kim Li.

"Excuse me, ma'am" I said, trying to get my server's attention. I said it again a little louder above the noise of the customers in the restaurant. This time she heard me, turned and mouthed "I'll be right there."

"Yes ma'am," she said as she returned to my table.

"I don't drink coffee. I think this was meant for another table." I said as I moved the coffee in her direction. The tiramisu looked absolutely divine. If she left it on my table any longer, I was going to taste it.

"Okay, I'll try to find out which table this belongs to," she interrupted, while scanning the restaurant to see who the actual recipient might be.

"Wait, just a moment please," I said, holding up my hand to stop her from leaving. "I noticed that my bill shows a zero balance but I haven't paid yet." The waitress picked up my ticket and briefly looked at the contents.

"Your meal was on the house, ma'am."

How can my meal be on the house?, I thought to myself. I looked around the restaurant trying to locate Kim Li. I knew she would be able to explain what was going on. I bet you this was some sort of joke. The Thursday trucker was trying to trick me into leaving the restaurant without paying. I had become so obsessed over the Thursday trucker that I now attributed pretty much any type of mischief or disorder to him. I was so caught up in the moment that I neglected to hear the waitress speaking to me.

"Ma'am?, Ma'am are you all right?"

"Yes of course. I just don't understand why my bill is zero." I said still pointing to the piece of paper in her hand.

"Ma'am, on the house means that it's free," The waitress said, speaking so slowly as if to emphasize her point. What she didn't realize was I didn't want to speak to her. I didn't want her trying to explain to me what 'on the house' meant. What I wanted was for her to find Kim Li, someone who would easily be able to explain what was going on.

"Look, I understand what on the house means. I just want to know who authorized my free meal." I knew enough about restaurants to know that only an owner or supervisor could authorize a free meal. Clearly, this young lady did understand what I wanted. My thoughts again were clearly etched on my face. So much so that even the waitress could read my mind.

"Don't worry, the owner okayed it". The waitress smiled and cleared the plates from my table.

I was still puzzled. Who was the owner? Why were they compelled to give me a free meal? Do they think I couldn't afford pay!? How insulting! I paused for a second and thought to myself about the white envelope safely hidden in my portable safe in the back of my truck. I sighed. I was doing it again. I was overthinking the issue. I took in two deep breaths and let them out. I took in a third one and released it to calm me down. This was probably nothing more than a kind gesture by the owner perhaps in hopes of getting my return business.

"Well, that was very kind of him. Please tell him I said thank you. I'll be sure to visit again." I said as I lay the five dollar tip on the table.

"Him? Who's him?" The waitress asked.

"The owner," I replied. The waitress giggled.

"The owner is a 'she'," the waitress laughed, picking up the five dollars from the table. Times must be tough. Usually a waiter or waitress will wait until I leave the table to pick up a tip. Not this one. I was curious as to who the owner was.

"Who is she? I don't think I've met her." I knew something was amiss when the waitress gave me a puzzled look. It was the same look Kim Li had given me earlier when she thought there was something wrong with me.

"She's right there," the waitress said, pointing to a table in the northwest corner of the restaurant. "It's Ms. Kim Li."

CHAPTER EIGHT

After I left the restaurant, I stopped by the roadside market to pick up some veggies to munch on. That was three hours ago. Now, I was busy trying to get to sleep with no success; seems like this place was full of mysteries and peculiarities. The first one was definitely the Thursday trucker. But now Kim Li. She didn't tell me she owned a restaurant. Kim Li didn't act like any restaurant owners I knew. And if she did, why was she working in the restaurant next to Connie's Motel? More importantly why was I bothered by it? Try as I might I could not quiet my mind. I sat up on the side of the bed. I'd come here to try and clear my head. With so much going on to distract me, I spent more time in other folks' business and hadn't given much time to deal with my own. I was restless again.

I felt a strong urge to get dressed and go over to the restaurant and ask what's going on. Then it dawned on me that's exactly what I'd expect me to do. The full moon was again

playing peekaboo through the opening in my
curtain. For some reason, I didn't feel like doing
what was expected anymore. I have to get back
to the reason why I was at Connie's Motel in
the first place. Two full moons had come and
gone and really nothing had changed. If I had
been a character in a movie or novel by now I
would've read reached some epiphany. I had
not.

James said that I start a lot of projects
but only finished a few of them. He was right.
James was right about a lot of things lately and
he wasn't even here to tell me. I turned from
the curtain and looked over to the desk. I had
several blank pieces of paper stacked on the
desk in preparation for writing my great
masterpiece. I walked over to the desk and sat
down. I picked up several sheets of blank paper.
I closed my eyes for my visualization exercise.
This time I could not see the grass covered in
white lilies. I opened my eyes and stared at the
papers. I realized my written masterpiece would
not be forthcoming tonight. I was restless. Kim
Li owned her own restaurant. She was a
businesswoman. What did I own? Nothing! I
have nothing to show for my work. I was still

restless.

I loaded up my one suitcase with my clothes, toiletries and the few items that I had purchased since coming to Connie's Motel. When I got restless it was time for me to travel. I looked around the room. I fought so fiercely to stay here now I felt like it was time for me to go. I needed to go somewhere. Some might call it running but I had to go where I was moved. Something inside of me took hold. The restlessness and the itching on the bottom of my right foot were all indicators that I need to go.

I doubled checked my motel room making sure I had loaded everything in the truck. I had acquired more stuff since coming to Connie's Motel. I left a note with $100 left on the bed.

Yes, Kim Li, I did enjoy the room. Thanks for the tea. Room 102. I closed the door behind me. I walked over to the motel office. Once again, John had forgotten to lock the office door. I walked inside and left a note for him as well which read *"Thank you, Room 102."* I put the note and my room key on top of John's keyboard. I didn't look back.

I drove for a couple of hours. I saw the sign, "Exit 169 here". I had a full tank of gas so there really was no need for me to stop. But, it was time for me to take care of some personal unfinished business at a particular roadside gas station. I pulled into the same stall as the first time. I got out and locked my truck. This time I wasn't afraid. I went inside. The layout of the store was the same but the feel of the place was distinctively different.

"Hello?" I called expecting to see Jim with his polo shirt and creased pants. Instead, it was the Thursday trucker. "What are you doing here?" I asked. I wonder what he'd done with Jim.

"It's a free country. I can travel where I please," the Thursday trucker said as he tipped his hat towards me. There he goes again pretending to be a gentleman. I wasn't fooled; I knew better. I worried about Kim Li. She couldn't see it, but the truth of the man was cleverly disguised behind a chiseled chin, perfect white teeth, and a pair of form fitting jeans.

I needed to keep my thoughts focused. It has been way too long since I've known the comfort of the arms of a man. My mind was playing tricks on me. The Thursday trucker was about as enticing as a cup of apple cider vinegar. I stopped here for a specific reason, to see Jim. I wasn't going to be derailed from my mission by the Thursday trucker's antics.

I looked around the store for Jim. Except for me and the Thursday trucker, the gas station was empty. Maybe he was cleaning the bathrooms.

"Who are you looking for?" The Thursday trucker asked as he walked up behind me. I was not comfortable with him standing so close to me. However the aisles were too small for me to turn around without bumping into him.

"I'm looking for someone," I responded

"Well, I'm the only one here," the Thursday trucker said. I could feel the heat of his stare on my back. He was trying to figure out which one of us was the craziest, him or me.

"Well, you weren't the one here the last I came through," I shot back. This was ridiculous. Here I was having an argument with the Thursday trucker and my back was turned to him. I could see the absurdity of the situation reflected in the glass doors of the ice cooler in front of me. I pretended I was looking for chips. This allowed me to walk further down the aisle so that I could turn around and face him. I don't know why but the Thursday trucker always kept me on edge. I really think I'm allergic to him, because no matter what day or time it is I always have a bad reaction. I hadn't planned on telling him why I was there but maybe he might know when Jim would be working again.

"You wouldn't happen to know when Jim will be working again?" I asked. Jim had helped me that night bringing me those 10 gallons of gas. I wanted to repay him at least financially.

"Jim, did you say?" The Thursday trucker asked.

"Yes, I need to give him something," I said. I don't know why I always felt the need to explain myself around the Thursday trucker. My original plan was to simply find out Jim's schedule. I could return and pay back the money for the ten gallons of gas. Instead, I spilled my guts to the Thursday trucker of all people.

"Jim was nice enough to help me out with some gas a while ago. I wanted to pay him back." The Thursday trucker looked at me as if he was trying to find my soul. I felt intrigued, but I did not like it. I wanted to be repulsed by him. That was safer. The Thursday trucker was intoxicating, but I wasn't going to take a drink.

"Here's the $20.98 for the gas," I said, placing the envelope in the Thursday trucker's hand. "Please make sure Jim gets it." The Thursday trucker did not take his eyes off me, not even to look at the envelope in his hand. He continued to watch me while he folded the envelope and put it in his left shirt pocket.

"Now you'll make sure he gets that when you see him, right?" I asked. I was still unsure of the Thursday trucker's intent.

"Yes, when I see him, I'll make sure he

gets it," Thursday trucker said, getting misty eyed. I was surprised by his display of emotion. As cruel as the Thursday Trucker was to me, I didn't think he had tear ducts. I debated whether I'd made the right decision giving the money to the Thursday trucker. It was only $20.98, not a significant amount. So, if the Thursday trucker kept it for himself, so be it, but it was the principle of the matter. I even considered whether I should ask him for the money back, but didn't want to appear rude. Instead, I turned around and went to the restroom. You never know where the next pit stop might be.

The bathroom was clean but it was not the same. The slender lavender vase was replaced by a woven basket which held three unopened roles of bathroom tissue. The paper towel dispenser had been exchanged for an automatic hand dryer; a model which I detested. Clearly, the owner assumed that everyone washed their hands. A foam dispenser with an unscented liquid soap was a poor substitute for the previous over-sized coconut-shea soap bottle. The bathroom was functional. It was a gas station restroom. I used the tail of my shirt to open the door. I would not be stopping here again. I almost ran into the Thursday trucker as I emerged from the bathroom.

"I was going to send in the cavalry to find you. I thought you might have gotten lost in there," Thursday trucker smiled behind the devilish white teeth.

"Just be sure that Jim gets that," I said, tapping the Thursday Trucker's shirt pocket as I passed by him. I headed out the door. The Thursday trucker was trying to say something to me that I did not have the desire nor the time to listen too.

I was about 70 miles from my destination. The scenery had become familiar to me about 30 miles back. Though this time I wasn't afraid. When I left here last I didn't know which way I should turn, left or right. Now, I know.

EPILOGUE

I pulled into the driveway. I was in no hurry to get out of my truck. I left here in anger and confusion, determined never to return. And yet, here I was back where it all started. I leaned my head against the steering wheel. There was no point in just sitting in the truck. Besides, if I stayed much longer my neighbors would be coming over to see what was wrong. The elderly couple that lived directly across the street saw everything. Those two knew who came in and who went out, what vehicle that person drove, and the state their license plate was issued in.

It could be intrusive and annoying at times. But, having those two always watching had its rewards. We had no crime. The worst thing that had been recorded in our neighborhood was last year when the young boy who lived two doors down, knocked out a window with his new model custom-built helicopter.

I had been lollygagging long enough. I know they saw me because the curtain that was open a moment ago was now shut. My lawn looked as if it had just been cut. My flowers had been pruned and the flower bed had fresh mulch. I could tell by the smell. If I didn't know better I would've thought someone had been living here.

I lifted the edge of the welcome mat to retrieve the key underneath. I'd left it there along with a note for James. Instead of the key I felt plastic. I pulled the mat further back to find a small plastic storage bag containing a key and note inside. I picked up the storage bag and straightened the mat. I took the note out and read it. "The home is yours. James."

I sat down on the porch swing. I read the note again. "How can this be a home without you, James?" I asked the wind. I took a deep breath and let it out. James! James! I spent too much of my time thinking about him. Well no more! I wasn't some lovesick kid. I wasn't going to keep mulling over James. This time I wasn't going to let my pride get in the way of a major blessing. This may not be a home but it was a great looking house. I shoved the piece of paper back in the storage bag, unlocked the door, and went inside. I closed the large oak wood door behind me. The memories of what used to be all came flooding back. I pressed my hands against my face. No, I didn't want to recall. I wanted to forget.

I promptly pushed back against the surge of emotions trying to overwhelm me. I would not give in to reliving what used to be. That would do nothing for me now. I thought about Kim Li. She was a businesswoman with something to show. I wanted to be the same. I did not want my living to be in vain, wasting or hiding away in some obscure roadside motel room.

Over the next hour, I continue to wrestle with memories and emotions that were trying to capture me and force me to feel. I refused and remained strong. I opened all the doors and windows. I wanted new air to flood the house. I wanted to clear the space of `what ifs' and what could've been. I paused for a moment to listen to the sound of the curtains popping in the wind. I felt the hairs on my arm prickle in response to the cool breeze flowing through every room. I closed my eyes. As strong as the wind was it could not erase everything, but I still tried.

I opened my eyes. I slowly walked through each room touching the furniture, the bed, the window sills, and the pictures still hanging on the wall; then finally returned to the kitchen. The house was spotless. As the breeze continued to flow through the house, I caught the faint scent of fresh lavender. I smiled. I felt something I hadn't felt in years. I felt peace. Out of the corner of my eye I spotted something familiar. Fresh white lilies were sitting in a lavender vase on the breakfast table. It looked as if the house had been prepared and had been waiting for someone to come home. It was waiting for me.

OTHER JACQUINITA A. ROSE TITLES

When Dreams Finally Come (Her Heart Heals Quietly Book 2)

Stained Glass Windows (Her Heart Heals Quietly Book 3)

Her Heart Heals Quietly: The Series Books 1 - 3

Shhh, Grown Folks Is Talking

Faith Has Conquered Fear

A Pressing Comb Saved Me From...

Good Respectable People (A Petite Fiction)

Brushing Mama's Hair (A Petite Fiction)

Daddy, Please Call (A Petite Fiction)

A New Math Attitude (Changing the Way You Think About Your Math Success)

R.U.D.A.R™(Read, Understand, Do, Apply, Retain)

7 Easy Moves For Solving Any Word Problem

10 Tips For Successful Homework

3 Basic Steps For Understanding Any Theorem, Property, or Rule

ABOUT THE AUTHOR

Jacquinita A. Rose enjoys writing short stories, flash fiction, inspirational fiction and nonfiction, novels, and how-to-for-math-success books.

Jacquinita is currently working on her fifth novel.

www.ingramcontent.com/pod-product-compliance
Lightning Source LLC
Chambersburg PA
CBHW020510030426
42337CB00011B/316